AT THE LIBRARY

Heather Alexander

Illustrated by Ipek Konak

Kane Miller
A DIVISION OF EDC PUBLISHING

A library is a place filled with stories and information.

There's probably a library in or near your town. Have you ever been to a library?

Shine a flashlight behind the page or hold it up to the light to see what's happening at the library. Discover a world of great surprises.

A library is a place that helps you learn. Inside the library, there are A LOT of books! Libraries are free, and everyone is welcome.

A man is reading the paper. Who else is using the library today?

They are all enj
the library

If you were in a library and you had a question, whom would you ask?

The librarian! Librarians know all about the library and will help you find a good book or the information you need.

Whom is this librarian helping?

An avid reader!

He wants to take some books home. He hands over his library card so that the librarian can scan the books and check them out for him.

No loud talking or making noise.

Visitors to the library should be quiet and respectful. Many people use the library to study or do work.

Shhh!

In libraries, fiction books are organized alphabetically by the author's last name. Nonfiction books are numbered and are part of the Dewey decimal classification system.

Do you know the difference between nonfiction and fiction?

Fiction is made up—it comes
from the author's imagination.

Nonfiction is information that is true.
It can be about people's lives or
an event that really happened.

You can have a lot of fun at the library. It's not always a quiet place. Sometimes libraries have special shows.

What's behind the curtain?

Puppets are behind the curtain!

Snap!

These children are
watching a puppet show.

It's story time at the library and one girl has brought a special friend. He's quiet, very soft, and loves bedtime stories.

Who is he?

Her teddy bear!

Some libraries have special areas just
for children, with comfortable seats,
cushions and toys. Children can play with
the library toys or bring their own along.

There is a long line of people waiting in this library.

What are they waiting for?

They are waiting to have their own books signed by the author!

Some libraries organize book signings. Authors sign the books and often read a few pages for their fans.

In a library, you borrow books and return them a little while later. Some libraries have self-checkout machines for borrowers to use.

How does this girl use the machine, and how many books is she borrowing?

She uses the scanner to scan her card,
then she scans her books. At the end,
a receipt is printed out that tells
her when to bring back her books.

Now she can enjoy them!

The girl comes back to the library one week later. She drops her books in the "return slot" in the wall.

Where did the books go?

All the books land in bins like this one.

Swoosh!

Later, a librarian or a library helper
will put them back on the shelves.

Life is full of questions, but where can you go for answers? A library is the perfect place; it can help you learn all sorts of things.

what is this boy looking at?

The world!

There are globes, computers,
dictionaries, atlases, newspapers
and much more in a library.

Do you know which animal has the largest eyes? Or how many bones there are in the human body?

These children are using the library computers to find the answers. Do you know what they are?

The giant squid has the largest eyes.

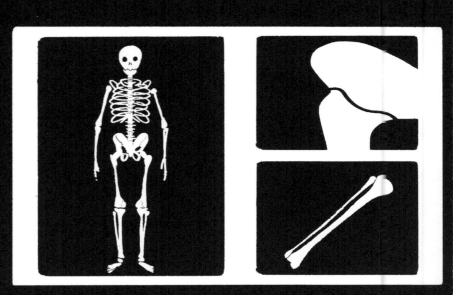

The adult human body has 206 bones.

This library has brought in a surprise guest.
The children will be able to read to him
after story time, but he seems to be hiding.

Can you spot him?

There he is! He's hiding under the rug.

Some libraries bring in dogs like this
one to encourage children to read
out loud and build their confidence.

WOOF!

What if a family lives very far away from a library? Some libraries have a special truck called a bookmobile, which can be driven to these places.

Can you see
what's inside?

There are toys, movies and lots
and lots of books, of course!

The Library of Congress in Washington, D.C., is the largest library in the world. It has a whopping 838 miles of bookshelves! This library has some very special items and collections.

What do you think these children are looking at?

They are looking at two of the
Library of Congress's special items:

The palm print of
Amelia Earhart. She
was the first woman
to fly solo across
the Atlantic Ocean.

Thomas Jefferson's
vanilla ice cream
recipe. He was the
third president of
the United States.

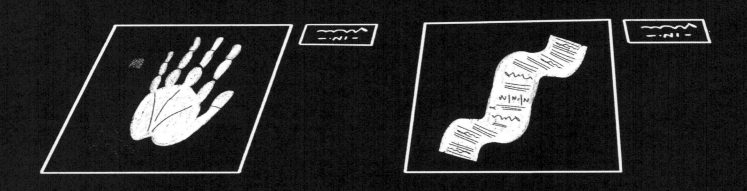

Not all libraries are big. A family has built a small wooden box and placed it outside their house.

What will this boy find inside?

"Take a book, leave a book" is how it works.
When you take a book, you're asked to leave
one of your own, so there's always a book
for the next person to read.

This book is almost done. What will you read next? A fiction book? Or how about a book about planes and trains? Visit the library and find more great books!

There's more...

Libraries around the world contain some of the most special and unique books, items and collections. Here are some of the brilliant books, cuddly companions and creepy collections on display.

Old King Cole   This is the smallest book in the Library of Congress. It is about the same size as the period at the end of this sentence.

Winnie the Pooh   The real stuffed bear that inspired the author A. A. Milne to write his famous stories is housed by the New York Public Library.

Mark Twain Project   Many libraries and organizations also have digital libraries that people can access online. The University of California, Berkeley, has a digital library of the writer Mark Twain's personal letters, notes and photographs that people can read and look at for free.

Magic collection   Princeton University Library has a special collection all about magic. The collection is made up of books, photographs and scrapbooks. Many of the books are very old and rare.

The contents of Abraham Lincoln's pockets

The Library of Congress has a collection of all of the things Abraham Lincoln had in his pockets the day he died. They include a handkerchief with his name stitched in red, a pocketknife and two pairs of glasses.

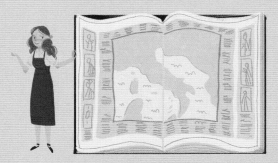

Klencke Atlas

This is the largest atlas in the world. Measuring 5 ft. 9 in. high and 6 ft. 3 in. wide, it is taller than many adults. It belongs to the British Library in London, UK.

Snow globe collection

A library at the University of Cincinnati holds a vast collection of striking snow globes displayed around the library for visitors to enjoy.

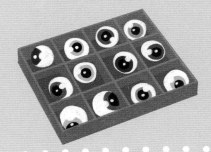

Eyeballs

Duke University in North Carolina has a gruesome medical collection, including a range of prosthetic glass eyeballs that students and researchers can inspect.

Seed library

The Vancouver Public Library in Vancouver, Canada, has a seed library where visitors can take, donate and trade seeds to grow in their gardens.

First American Edition 2019
Kane Miller, A Division of EDC Publishing

Copyright © 2019 Quarto Publishing plc

For information contact:
Kane Miller, A Division of EDC Publishing
PO Box 470663
Tulsa, OK 74147-0663
www.kanemiller.com
www.edcpub.com
www.usbornebooksandmore.com

Library of Congress Control Number: 2018942380

Printed in China

ISBN: 978-1-61067-823-0

2 3 4 5 6 7 8 9 10